DAILY PLANNER

NAME

ADDRESS

PHONE

EMAIL

DATE	WEEK

MY GOALS | DONE

.... ☐
.... ☐
.... ☐
.... ☐
.... ☐
.... ☐
.... ☐
.... ☐

MY STRATEGIES

....
....
....
....
....
....
....
....

SHOPPING LIST

....
....
....
....
....
....

MY TASKS

....
....
....
....
....
....
....

MY TASKS

....
....
....
....
....
....
....

MY TASKS

....
....
....
....
....
....
....

BFAST	LUNCH	DINNER

SNACKS	EXERCISE

OUTFIT

IMPORTANT NOTE

BFAST	LUNCH	DINNER

SNACKS	EXERCISE

OUTFIT

IMPORTANT NOTE

BFAST	LUNCH	DINNER

SNACKS	EXERCISE

OUTFIT

IMPORTANT NOTE

THU

MY TASKS

....
....
....
....
....
....
....

BFAST	LUNCH	DINNER

SNACKS	EXERCISE

OUTFIT

IMPORTANT NOTE

THINGS I SHOULD TAKE NOTES OF

....
....
....
....
....
....
....
....
....

FRI

MY TASKS

....
....
....
....
....
....

BFAST	LUNCH	DINNER

SNACKS	EXERCISE

OUTFIT

IMPORTANT NOTE

....
....
....
....
....
....

SAT

MY TASKS

....
....
....
....

BFAST	LUNCH	DINNER

OUTFIT

SUN

MY TASKS

....
....
....
....

BFAST	LUNCH	DINNER

OUTFIT

WEEKLY REVIEW

NO. OF GOALS ACHIEVED?..............
LESSONS LEARNED?

....
....
....

HIGHLIGHTS THIS WEEK?

....
....

AM I HAPPY WITH THE RESULT?

DATE	WEEK

MY GOALS   DONE

- .... ☐
- .... ☐
- .... ☐
- .... ☐
- .... ☐
- .... ☐
- .... ☐
- .... ☐

MY TASKS

- ....
- ....
- ....
- ....
- ....
- ....
- ....

BFAST	LUNCH	DINNER

SNACKS	EXERCISE

OUTFIT

IMPORTANT NOTE

MY STRATEGIES

- ....
- ....
- ....
- ....
- ....
- ....
- ....

MY TASKS

- ....
- ....
- ....
- ....
- ....
- ....
- ....

BFAST	LUNCH	DINNER

SNACKS	EXERCISE

OUTFIT

IMPORTANT NOTE

SHOPPING LIST

- ....
- ....
- ....
- ....
- ....
- ....
- ....

MY TASKS

- ....
- ....
- ....
- ....
- ....
- ....
- ....

BFAST	LUNCH	DINNER

SNACKS	EXERCISE

OUTFIT

IMPORTANT NOTE

THU

MY TASKS

....
....
....
....
....
....
....
....
....

BFAST	LUNCH	DINNER

SNACKS	EXERCISE

OUTFIT

IMPORTANT NOTE

THINGS I SHOULD TAKE NOTES OF

....
....
....
....
....
....
....

FRI

MY TASKS

....
....
....
....
....
....
....
....
....

BFAST	LUNCH	DINNER

SNACKS	EXERCISE

OUTFIT

IMPORTANT NOTE

....
....
....
....
....
....

SAT

MY TASKS

....
....
....
....

BFAST	LUNCH	DINNER

OUTFIT

SUN

MY TASKS

....
....
....
....

BFAST	LUNCH	DINNER

OUTFIT

WEEKLY REVIEW

NO. OF GOALS ACHIEVED?..........
LESSONS LEARNED?

....
....
....

HIGHLIGHTS THIS WEEK?

....
....
....

AM I HAPPY WITH THE RESULT?

DATE	WEEK

MY GOALS / DONE

- .... ☐
- .... ☐
- .... ☐
- .... ☐
- .... ☐
- .... ☐
- .... ☐
- .... ☐

MY TASKS

- ....
- ....
- ....
- ....
- ....
- ....

BFAST	LUNCH	DINNER

SNACKS	EXERCISE

OUTFIT

IMPORTANT NOTE

MY STRATEGIES

- ....
- ....
- ....
- ....
- ....
- ....
- ....
- ....

MY TASKS

- ....
- ....
- ....
- ....
- ....
- ....

BFAST	LUNCH	DINNER

SNACKS	EXERCISE

OUTFIT

IMPORTANT NOTE

SHOPPING LIST

MY TASKS

- ....
- ....
- ....
- ....
- ....
- ....

BFAST	LUNCH	DINNER

SNACKS	EXERCISE

OUTFIT

IMPORTANT NOTE

MY TASKS

THU

....
....
....
....
....
....
....

BFAST	LUNCH	DINNER

SNACKS	EXERCISE

OUTFIT

IMPORTANT NOTE

THINGS I SHOULD TAKE NOTES OF

....
....
....
....
....
....
....

MY TASKS

FRI

....
....
....
....
....
....
....

BFAST	LUNCH	DINNER

SNACKS	EXERCISE

OUTFIT

IMPORTANT NOTE

....
....
....
....
....
....
....

MY TASKS

SAT

....
....
....
....

BFAST	LUNCH	DINNER

OUTFIT

MY TASKS

SUN

....
....
....
....

BFAST	LUNCH	DINNER

OUTFIT

WEEKLY REVIEW

NO. OF GOALS ACHIEVED?............
LESSONS LEARNED?

....
....
....

HIGHLIGHTS THIS WEEK?

....
....
....

AM I HAPPY WITH THE RESULT?

DATE	WEEK

MY GOALS   DONE

.... ☐
.... ☐
.... ☐
.... ☐
.... ☐
.... ☐
.... ☐
.... ☐

MY TASKS

BFAST	LUNCH	DINNER

SNACKS	EXERCISE

OUTFIT

IMPORTANT NOTE

MY STRATEGIES

MY TASKS

BFAST	LUNCH	DINNER

SNACKS	EXERCISE

OUTFIT

IMPORTANT NOTE

SHOPPING LIST

MY TASKS

BFAST	LUNCH	DINNER

SNACKS	EXERCISE

OUTFIT

IMPORTANT NOTE

MY TASKS

THU

....
....
....
....
....
....
....

BFAST	LUNCH	DINNER

SNACKS	EXERCISE

OUTFIT

IMPORTANT NOTE

THINGS I SHOULD TAKE NOTES OF

....
....
....
....
....
....
....
....
....
....

MY TASKS

FRI

....
....
....
....
....
....
....

BFAST	LUNCH	DINNER

SNACKS	EXERCISE

OUTFIT

IMPORTANT NOTE

....
....
....
....
....
....
....

MY TASKS

SAT

....
....
....
....

BFAST	LUNCH	DINNER

OUTFIT

MY TASKS

SUN

....
....
....
....

BFAST	LUNCH	DINNER

OUTFIT

WEEKLY REVIEW

NO. OF GOALS ACHIEVED?............
LESSONS LEARNED?

....
....
....

HIGHLIGHTS THIS WEEK?

....
....
....

AM I HAPPY WITH THE RESULT?

DATE	WEEK

MY GOALS — DONE

.... ☐
.... ☐
.... ☐
.... ☐
.... ☐
.... ☐
.... ☐
.... ☐
.... ☐

MY STRATEGIES

....
....
....
....
....
....
....
....

SHOPPING LIST

....
....
....
....
....
....
....

MY TASKS

....
....
....
....
....
....
....
....

BFAST	LUNCH	DINNER

SNACKS	EXERCISE

OUTFIT

IMPORTANT NOTE

MY TASKS

....
....
....
....
....
....
....
....

BFAST	LUNCH	DINNER

SNACKS	EXERCISE

OUTFIT

IMPORTANT NOTE

MY TASKS

....
....
....
....
....
....
....
....

BFAST	LUNCH	DINNER

SNACKS	EXERCISE

OUTFIT

IMPORTANT NOTE

THU

MY TASKS

....
....
....
....
....
....
....
....

BFAST	LUNCH	DINNER

SNACKS	EXERCISE

OUTFIT

IMPORTANT NOTE

THINGS I SHOULD TAKE NOTES OF

....
....
....
....
....
....
....

FRI

MY TASKS

....
....
....
....
....
....
....
....

BFAST	LUNCH	DINNER

SNACKS	EXERCISE

OUTFIT

IMPORTANT NOTE

....
....
....
....
....
....

SAT

MY TASKS

....
....
....
....
....

BFAST	LUNCH	DINNER

OUTFIT

SUN

MY TASKS

....
....
....
....
....

BFAST	LUNCH	DINNER

OUTFIT

WEEKLY REVIEW

NO. OF GOALS ACHIEVED?..............
LESSONS LEARNED?

....
....
....

HIGHLIGHTS THIS WEEK?

....
....
....

AM I HAPPY WITH THE RESULT?

DATE	WEEK

MY GOALS — DONE

- .... ☐
- .... ☐
- .... ☐
- .... ☐
- .... ☐
- .... ☐
- .... ☐
- .... ☐
- .... ☐

MY TASKS

- ....
- ....
- ....
- ....
- ....
- ....
- ....
- ....

BFAST	LUNCH	DINNER

SNACKS	EXERCISE

OUTFIT

IMPORTANT NOTE

MY STRATEGIES

- ....
- ....
- ....
- ....
- ....
- ....
- ....

MY TASKS

- ....
- ....
- ....
- ....
- ....
- ....
- ....

BFAST	LUNCH	DINNER

SNACKS	EXERCISE

OUTFIT

IMPORTANT NOTE

SHOPPING LIST

MY TASKS

- ....
- ....
- ....
- ....
- ....
- ....
- ....

BFAST	LUNCH	DINNER

SNACKS	EXERCISE

OUTFIT

IMPORTANT NOTE

MY TASKS (THU)

....
....
....
....
....
....
....

BFAST	LUNCH	DINNER

SNACKS	EXERCISE

OUTFIT

IMPORTANT NOTE

THINGS I SHOULD TAKE NOTES OF

....
....
....
....
....
....
....
....
....
....

MY TASKS (FRI)

....
....
....
....
....
....
....

BFAST	LUNCH	DINNER

SNACKS	EXERCISE

OUTFIT

IMPORTANT NOTE

....
....
....
....
....

MY TASKS (SAT)

....
....
....
....

BFAST	LUNCH	DINNER

OUTFIT

MY TASKS (SUN)

....
....
....
....

BFAST	LUNCH	DINNER

OUTFIT

WEEKLY REVIEW

NO. OF GOALS ACHIEVED?.............
LESSONS LEARNED?

....
....
....

HIGHLIGHTS THIS WEEK?

....
....

AM I HAPPY WITH THE RESULT?

DATE	WEEK

MY GOALS — DONE

- .... ☐
- .... ☐
- .... ☐
- .... ☐
- .... ☐
- .... ☐
- .... ☐
- .... ☐

MY TASKS

- ....
- ....
- ....
- ....
- ....
- ....
- ....
- ....

BFAST	LUNCH	DINNER

SNACKS	EXERCISE

OUTFIT

IMPORTANT NOTE

MY STRATEGIES

- ....
- ....
- ....
- ....
- ....
- ....
- ....
- ....

MY TASKS

- ....
- ....
- ....
- ....
- ....
- ....
- ....

BFAST	LUNCH	DINNER

SNACKS	EXERCISE

OUTFIT

IMPORTANT NOTE

SHOPPING LIST

....	....
....	....
....	....
....	....
....	....
....	....
....	....

MY TASKS

- ....
- ....
- ....
- ....
- ....
- ....
- ....

BFAST	LUNCH	DINNER

SNACKS	EXERCISE

OUTFIT

IMPORTANT NOTE

MY TASKS

THU

BFAST	LUNCH	DINNER

SNACKS	EXERCISE

OUTFIT

IMPORTANT NOTE

THINGS I SHOULD TAKE NOTES OF

MY TASKS

FRI

BFAST	LUNCH	DINNER

SNACKS	EXERCISE

OUTFIT

IMPORTANT NOTE

MY TASKS

SAT

BFAST	LUNCH	DINNER

OUTFIT

MY TASKS

SUN

BFAST	LUNCH	DINNER

OUTFIT

WEEKLY REVIEW

NO. OF GOALS ACHIEVED?

LESSONS LEARNED?

HIGHLIGHTS THIS WEEK?

AM I HAPPY WITH THE RESULT?

DATE	WEEK

MY GOALS / DONE

.... ☐
.... ☐
.... ☐
.... ☐
.... ☐
.... ☐
.... ☐
.... ☐
.... ☐

MY STRATEGIES

....
....
....
....
....
....
....
....

SHOPPING LIST

....
....
....
....
....
....
....

MY TASKS

....
....
....
....
....
....
....
....

MY TASKS

....
....
....
....
....
....

MY TASKS

....
....
....
....
....
....

BFAST	LUNCH	DINNER

SNACKS	EXERCISE

OUTFIT

IMPORTANT NOTE

BFAST	LUNCH	DINNER

SNACKS	EXERCISE

OUTFIT

IMPORTANT NOTE

BFAST	LUNCH	DINNER

SNACKS	EXERCISE

OUTFIT

IMPORTANT NOTE

THU

MY TASKS

....
....
....
....
....
....
....

BFAST	LUNCH	DINNER

SNACKS	EXERCISE

OUTFIT

IMPORTANT NOTE

THINGS I SHOULD TAKE NOTES OF

....
....
....
....
....

FRI

MY TASKS

....
....
....
....
....
....

BFAST	LUNCH	DINNER

SNACKS	EXERCISE

OUTFIT

IMPORTANT NOTE

....
....
....
....

SAT

MY TASKS

....
....
....
....

BFAST	LUNCH	DINNER

OUTFIT

SUN

MY TASKS

....
....
....
....

BFAST	LUNCH	DINNER

OUTFIT

WEEKLY REVIEW

NO. OF GOALS ACHIEVED?..........
LESSONS LEARNED?
....
....
....

HIGHLIGHTS THIS WEEK?
....
....

AM I HAPPY WITH THE RESULT?

DATE	WEEK

MY GOALS — DONE

- .... ☐
- .... ☐
- .... ☐
- .... ☐
- .... ☐
- .... ☐
- .... ☐
- .... ☐

MY TASKS

- ....
- ....
- ....
- ....
- ....
- ....
- ....
- ....

BFAST	LUNCH	DINNER

SNACKS	EXERCISE

OUTFIT

IMPORTANT NOTE

MY STRATEGIES

- ....
- ....
- ....
- ....
- ....
- ....
- ....
- ....

MY TASKS

- ....
- ....
- ....
- ....
- ....
- ....
- ....
- ....

BFAST	LUNCH	DINNER

SNACKS	EXERCISE

OUTFIT

IMPORTANT NOTE

SHOPPING LIST

MY TASKS

- ....
- ....
- ....
- ....
- ....
- ....
- ....
- ....

BFAST	LUNCH	DINNER

SNACKS	EXERCISE

OUTFIT

IMPORTANT NOTE

MY TASKS

THU

....
....
....
....
....
....
....

BFAST	LUNCH	DINNER

SNACKS	EXERCISE

OUTFIT

IMPORTANT NOTE

THINGS I SHOULD TAKE NOTES OF

....
....
....
....
....
....
....

MY TASKS

FRI

....
....
....
....
....
....

BFAST	LUNCH	DINNER

SNACKS	EXERCISE

OUTFIT

IMPORTANT NOTE

....
....
....
....
....
....

MY TASKS

SAT

....
....
....
....

BFAST	LUNCH	DINNER

OUTFIT

MY TASKS

SUN

....
....
....
....

BFAST	LUNCH	DINNER

OUTFIT

WEEKLY REVIEW

NO. OF GOALS ACHIEVED?..............
LESSONS LEARNED?

....
....
....

HIGHLIGHTS THIS WEEK?

....
....
....

AM I HAPPY WITH THE RESULT?

DATE	WEEK

MY GOALS / DONE

	☐
....	☐
....	☐
....	☐
....	☐
....	☐
....	☐
....	☐
....	☐

MY TASKS

....
....
....
....
....
....
....
....

BFAST	LUNCH	DINNER

SNACKS	EXERCISE

OUTFIT

IMPORTANT NOTE

MY STRATEGIES

....
....
....
....
....
....
....

MY TASKS

....
....
....
....
....
....
....
....

BFAST	LUNCH	DINNER

SNACKS	EXERCISE

OUTFIT

IMPORTANT NOTE

SHOPPING LIST

MY TASKS

....
....
....
....
....
....
....
....

BFAST	LUNCH	DINNER

SNACKS	EXERCISE

OUTFIT

IMPORTANT NOTE

THU

MY TASKS

....
....
....
....
....
....
....
....
....

BFAST	LUNCH	DINNER

SNACKS	EXERCISE

OUTFIT

IMPORTANT NOTE

THINGS I SHOULD TAKE NOTES OF

....
....
....
....
....
....
....
....
....
....

FRI

MY TASKS

....
....
....
....
....
....
....
....
....

BFAST	LUNCH	DINNER

SNACKS	EXERCISE

OUTFIT

IMPORTANT NOTE

....
....
....
....
....
....

SAT

MY TASKS

....
....
....
....
....

BFAST	LUNCH	DINNER

OUTFIT

SUN

MY TASKS

....
....
....
....
....

BFAST	LUNCH	DINNER

OUTFIT

WEEKLY REVIEW

NO. OF GOALS ACHIEVED?..........
LESSONS LEARNED?

....
....
....

HIGHLIGHTS THIS WEEK?

....
....
....

AM I HAPPY WITH THE RESULT?

DATE	WEEK

MY GOALS — DONE

.... ☐
.... ☐
.... ☐
.... ☐
.... ☐
.... ☐
.... ☐
.... ☐

MY TASKS

....
....
....
....
....
....
....

BFAST	LUNCH	DINNER

SNACKS	EXERCISE

OUTFIT

IMPORTANT NOTE

MY STRATEGIES

....
....
....
....
....
....
....
....

MY TASKS

....
....
....
....
....
....
....

BFAST	LUNCH	DINNER

SNACKS	EXERCISE

OUTFIT

IMPORTANT NOTE

SHOPPING LIST

MY TASKS

....
....
....
....
....
....
....

BFAST	LUNCH	DINNER

SNACKS	EXERCISE

OUTFIT

IMPORTANT NOTE

THU

MY TASKS

....
....
....
....
....
....
....
....

BFAST	LUNCH	DINNER

SNACKS	EXERCISE

OUTFIT

IMPORTANT NOTE

THINGS I SHOULD TAKE NOTES OF

....
....
....
....
....
....
....
....
....
....
....
....
....
....

FRI

MY TASKS

....
....
....
....
....
....
....
....

BFAST	LUNCH	DINNER

SNACKS	EXERCISE

OUTFIT

IMPORTANT NOTE

SAT

MY TASKS

....
....
....
....

BFAST	LUNCH	DINNER

OUTFIT

SUN

MY TASKS

....
....
....
....

BFAST	LUNCH	DINNER

OUTFIT

WEEKLY REVIEW

NO. OF GOALS ACHIEVED? ....
LESSONS LEARNED?

....
....
....

HIGHLIGHTS THIS WEEK?

....
....
....

AM I HAPPY WITH THE RESULT?

DATE	WEEK

MY GOALS | DONE

- .... ☐
- .... ☐
- .... ☐
- .... ☐
- .... ☐
- .... ☐
- .... ☐
- .... ☐

MY TASKS

- ....
- ....
- ....
- ....
- ....
- ....

BFAST	LUNCH	DINNER

SNACKS	EXERCISE

OUTFIT

IMPORTANT NOTE

MY STRATEGIES

- ....
- ....
- ....
- ....
- ....
- ....
- ....

MY TASKS

- ....
- ....
- ....
- ....
- ....
- ....
- ....

BFAST	LUNCH	DINNER

SNACKS	EXERCISE

OUTFIT

IMPORTANT NOTE

SHOPPING LIST

MY TASKS

- ....
- ....
- ....
- ....
- ....
- ....
- ....

BFAST	LUNCH	DINNER

SNACKS	EXERCISE

OUTFIT

IMPORTANT NOTE

MY TASKS

THU

....
....
....
....
....
....
....

BFAST	LUNCH	DINNER

SNACKS	EXERCISE

OUTFIT

IMPORTANT NOTE

THINGS I SHOULD TAKE NOTES OF

....
....
....
....
....
....
....
....

MY TASKS

FRI

....
....
....
....
....
....
....

BFAST	LUNCH	DINNER

SNACKS	EXERCISE

OUTFIT

IMPORTANT NOTE

....
....
....
....
....

MY TASKS

SAT

....
....
....
....

BFAST	LUNCH	DINNER

OUTFIT

MY TASKS

SUN

....
....
....
....

BFAST	LUNCH	DINNER

OUTFIT

WEEKLY REVIEW

NO. OF GOALS ACHIEVED?.............
LESSONS LEARNED?

....
....
....

HIGHLIGHTS THIS WEEK?

....
....

AM I HAPPY WITH THE RESULT?

DATE	WEEK

MY GOALS   DONE

.... ☐
.... ☐
.... ☐
.... ☐
.... ☐
.... ☐
.... ☐
.... ☐
.... ☐

MY TASKS

....
....
....
....
....
....
....

BFAST	LUNCH	DINNER

SNACKS   EXERCISE

OUTFIT

IMPORTANT NOTE

MY STRATEGIES

....
....
....
....
....
....
....

MY TASKS

....
....
....
....
....
....
....

BFAST	LUNCH	DINNER

SNACKS   EXERCISE

OUTFIT

IMPORTANT NOTE

SHOPPING LIST

MY TASKS

....
....
....
....
....
....
....

BFAST	LUNCH	DINNER

SNACKS   EXERCISE

OUTFIT

IMPORTANT NOTE

MY TASKS

THU

BFAST   LUNCH   DINNER

SNACKS   EXERCISE

OUTFIT

IMPORTANT NOTE

THINGS I SHOULD TAKE NOTES OF

MY TASKS

FRI

BFAST   LUNCH   DINNER

SNACKS   EXERCISE

OUTFIT

IMPORTANT NOTE

MY TASKS

SAT

BFAST   LUNCH   DINNER

OUTFIT

MY TASKS

SUN

BFAST   LUNCH   DINNER

OUTFIT

WEEKLY REVIEW

NO. OF GOALS ACHIEVED?
LESSONS LEARNED?

HIGHLIGHTS THIS WEEK?

AM I HAPPY WITH THE RESULT?

DATE	WEEK

MY GOALS | DONE

.... ☐
.... ☐
.... ☐
.... ☐
.... ☐
.... ☐
.... ☐
.... ☐

MY STRATEGIES

....
....
....
....
....
....
....
....

SHOPPING LIST

....
....
....
....
....
....
....
....

MY TASKS

....
....
....
....
....
....
....

MY TASKS

....
....
....
....
....
....
....

MY TASKS

....
....
....
....
....
....
....

BFAST	LUNCH	DINNER

SNACKS | EXERCISE

OUTFIT

IMPORTANT NOTE

BFAST	LUNCH	DINNER

SNACKS | EXERCISE

OUTFIT

IMPORTANT NOTE

BFAST	LUNCH	DINNER

SNACKS | EXERCISE

OUTFIT

IMPORTANT NOTE

THU

MY TASKS

....
....
....
....
....
....
....

BFAST	LUNCH	DINNER

SNACKS	EXERCISE

OUTFIT

IMPORTANT NOTE

THINGS I SHOULD TAKE NOTES OF

....
....
....
....
....
....
....
....
....
....

FRI

MY TASKS

....
....
....
....
....
....
....

BFAST	LUNCH	DINNER

SNACKS	EXERCISE

OUTFIT

IMPORTANT NOTE

....
....
....
....
....
....

SAT

MY TASKS

....
....
....
....

BFAST	LUNCH	DINNER

OUTFIT

SUN

MY TASKS

....
....
....
....

BFAST	LUNCH	DINNER

OUTFIT

WEEKLY REVIEW

NO. OF GOALS ACHIEVED?..............
LESSONS LEARNED?

....
....
....

HIGHLIGHTS THIS WEEK?

....
....
....

AM I HAPPY WITH THE RESULT?

DATE	WEEK

MY GOALS   DONE

.... ☐
.... ☐
.... ☐
.... ☐
.... ☐
.... ☐
.... ☐
.... ☐

MY TASKS

....
....
....
....
....
....
....
....

BFAST	LUNCH	DINNER

SNACKS	EXERCISE

OUTFIT

IMPORTANT NOTE

MY STRATEGIES

....
....
....
....
....
....
....
....

MY TASKS

....
....
....
....
....
....
....
....

BFAST	LUNCH	DINNER

SNACKS	EXERCISE

OUTFIT

IMPORTANT NOTE

SHOPPING LIST

....
....
....
....
....
....
....
....

MY TASKS

....
....
....
....
....
....
....
....

BFAST	LUNCH	DINNER

SNACKS	EXERCISE

OUTFIT

IMPORTANT NOTE

THU

MY TASKS
....
....
....
....
....
....
....

BFAST | LUNCH | DINNER

SNACKS | EXERCISE

OUTFIT

IMPORTANT NOTE

THINGS I SHOULD TAKE NOTES OF
....
....
....
....
....
....
....
....
....

FRI

MY TASKS
....
....
....
....
....
....
....

BFAST | LUNCH | DINNER

SNACKS | EXERCISE

OUTFIT

IMPORTANT NOTE

....
....
....
....
....
....
....
....
....

SAT

MY TASKS
....
....
....
....

BFAST | LUNCH | DINNER

OUTFIT

SUN

MY TASKS
....
....
....
....

BFAST | LUNCH | DINNER

OUTFIT

WEEKLY REVIEW
NO. OF GOALS ACHIEVED?.........
LESSONS LEARNED?
....
....
....

HIGHLIGHTS THIS WEEK?
....
....

AM I HAPPY WITH THE RESULT?

DATE	WEEK

MY GOALS / DONE

- .... ☐
- .... ☐
- .... ☐
- .... ☐
- .... ☐
- .... ☐
- .... ☐
- .... ☐

MY TASKS

MON

- ....
- ....
- ....
- ....
- ....
- ....

BFAST	LUNCH	DINNER

SNACKS	EXERCISE

OUTFIT

IMPORTANT NOTE

MY STRATEGIES

- ....
- ....
- ....
- ....
- ....
- ....
- ....

MY TASKS

TUE

- ....
- ....
- ....
- ....
- ....
- ....

BFAST	LUNCH	DINNER

SNACKS	EXERCISE

OUTFIT

IMPORTANT NOTE

SHOPPING LIST

....	
....	
....	
....	
....	
....	
....	

MY TASKS

WED

- ....
- ....
- ....
- ....
- ....
- ....

BFAST	LUNCH	DINNER

SNACKS	EXERCISE

OUTFIT

IMPORTANT NOTE

MY TASKS

THU

BFAST	LUNCH	DINNER

SNACKS	EXERCISE

OUTFIT

IMPORTANT NOTE

THINGS I SHOULD TAKE NOTES OF

MY TASKS

FRI

BFAST	LUNCH	DINNER

SNACKS	EXERCISE

OUTFIT

IMPORTANT NOTE

MY TASKS

SAT

BFAST	LUNCH	DINNER

OUTFIT

MY TASKS

SUN

BFAST	LUNCH	DINNER

OUTFIT

WEEKLY REVIEW

NO. OF GOALS ACHIEVED?

LESSONS LEARNED?

HIGHLIGHTS THIS WEEK?

AM I HAPPY WITH THE RESULT?

DATE	WEEK

MY GOALS

DONE

- .... ☐
- .... ☐
- .... ☐
- .... ☐
- .... ☐
- .... ☐
- .... ☐
- .... ☐

MY STRATEGIES

- ....
- ....
- ....
- ....
- ....
- ....
- ....
- ....

SHOPPING LIST

MY TASKS

- ....
- ....
- ....
- ....
- ....
- ....
- ....
- ....

MON

BFAST	LUNCH	DINNER

SNACKS	EXERCISE

OUTFIT

IMPORTANT NOTE

MY TASKS

- ....
- ....
- ....
- ....
- ....
- ....
- ....
- ....

BFAST	LUNCH	DINNER

SNACKS	EXERCISE

OUTFIT

IMPORTANT NOTE

MY TASKS

- ....
- ....
- ....
- ....
- ....
- ....
- ....
- ....

WED

BFAST	LUNCH	DINNER

SNACKS	EXERCISE

OUTFIT

IMPORTANT NOTE

THU

MY TASKS

....
....
....
....
....
....
....
....

BFAST	LUNCH	DINNER

SNACKS	EXERCISE

OUTFIT

IMPORTANT NOTE

THINGS I SHOULD TAKE NOTES OF

....
....
....
....
....
....

FRI

MY TASKS

....
....
....
....
....
....
....

BFAST	LUNCH	DINNER

SNACKS	EXERCISE

OUTFIT

IMPORTANT NOTE

....
....
....
....
....
....

SAT

MY TASKS

....
....
....
....

BFAST	LUNCH	DINNER

OUTFIT

SUN

MY TASKS

....
....
....
....

BFAST	LUNCH	DINNER

OUTFIT

WEEKLY REVIEW

NO. OF GOALS ACHIEVED?..........
LESSONS LEARNED?

....
....
....

HIGHLIGHTS THIS WEEK?

....
....
....

AM I HAPPY WITH THE RESULT?

DATE	WEEK

MY GOALS
DONE

.... ☐
.... ☐
.... ☐
.... ☐
.... ☐
.... ☐
.... ☐
.... ☐
.... ☐

MY STRATEGIES

....
....
....
....
....
....
....
....

SHOPPING LIST

MY TASKS (MON)

....
....
....
....
....
....
....

BFAST	LUNCH	DINNER

SNACKS	EXERCISE

OUTFIT

IMPORTANT NOTE

MY TASKS (TUE)

....
....
....
....
....
....

BFAST	LUNCH	DINNER

SNACKS	EXERCISE

OUTFIT

IMPORTANT NOTE

MY TASKS (WED)

....
....
....
....
....
....

BFAST	LUNCH	DINNER

SNACKS	EXERCISE

OUTFIT

IMPORTANT NOTE

THU

MY TASKS

....
....
....
....
....
....
....

BFAST	LUNCH	DINNER

SNACKS	EXERCISE

OUTFIT

IMPORTANT NOTE

THINGS I SHOULD TAKE NOTES OF

....
....
....
....
....
....
....
....
....
....
....
....

FRI

MY TASKS

....
....
....
....
....
....
....

BFAST	LUNCH	DINNER

SNACKS	EXERCISE

OUTFIT

IMPORTANT NOTE

....
....
....
....
....
....

SAT

MY TASKS

....
....
....
....
....

BFAST	LUNCH	DINNER

OUTFIT

SUN

MY TASKS

....
....
....
....
....

BFAST	LUNCH	DINNER

OUTFIT

WEEKLY REVIEW

NO. OF GOALS ACHIEVED?................
LESSONS LEARNED?

....
....
....

HIGHLIGHTS THIS WEEK?

....
....
....

AM I HAPPY WITH THE RESULT?

DATE	WEEK

MY GOALS   DONE

- .... ☐
- .... ☐
- .... ☐
- .... ☐
- .... ☐
- .... ☐
- .... ☐
- .... ☐

MY STRATEGIES

- ....
- ....
- ....
- ....
- ....
- ....
- ....
- ....

SHOPPING LIST

MY TASKS

- ....
- ....
- ....
- ....
- ....
- ....
- ....

BFAST	LUNCH	DINNER

SNACKS	EXERCISE

OUTFIT

IMPORTANT NOTE

MY TASKS

- ....
- ....
- ....
- ....
- ....
- ....
- ....

BFAST	LUNCH	DINNER

SNACKS	EXERCISE

OUTFIT

IMPORTANT NOTE

MY TASKS

- ....
- ....
- ....
- ....
- ....
- ....
- ....

BFAST	LUNCH	DINNER

SNACKS	EXERCISE

OUTFIT

IMPORTANT NOTE

MY TASKS (THU)

- ....
- ....
- ....
- ....
- ....
- ....
- ....
- ....

BFAST	LUNCH	DINNER

SNACKS	EXERCISE

OUTFIT

IMPORTANT NOTE

THINGS I SHOULD TAKE NOTES OF

- ....
- ....
- ....
- ....
- ....
- ....
- ....
- ....
- ....
- ....
- ....
- ....

MY TASKS (FRI)

- ....
- ....
- ....
- ....
- ....
- ....
- ....
- ....

BFAST	LUNCH	DINNER

SNACKS	EXERCISE

OUTFIT

IMPORTANT NOTE

MY TASKS (SAT)

- ....
- ....
- ....
- ....

BFAST	LUNCH	DINNER

OUTFIT

MY TASKS (SUN)

- ....
- ....
- ....
- ....

BFAST	LUNCH	DINNER

OUTFIT

WEEKLY REVIEW

NO. OF GOALS ACHIEVED?..............
LESSONS LEARNED?

- ....
- ....
- ....

HIGHLIGHTS THIS WEEK?

- ....
- ....

AM I HAPPY WITH THE RESULT?

DATE	WEEK

MY GOALS — DONE

- -- ☐
- -- ☐
- -- ☐
- -- ☐
- -- ☐
- -- ☐
- -- ☐
- -- ☐

MY TASKS

- --
- --
- --
- --
- --
- --
- --

BFAST	LUNCH	DINNER

SNACKS	EXERCISE

OUTFIT

IMPORTANT NOTE

MY STRATEGIES

- --
- --
- --
- --
- --
- --
- --
- --

MY TASKS

- --
- --
- --
- --
- --
- --
- --
- --

BFAST	LUNCH	DINNER

SNACKS	EXERCISE

OUTFIT

IMPORTANT NOTE

SHOPPING LIST

- ---------------- | ----------------
- ---------------- | ----------------
- ---------------- | ----------------
- ---------------- | ----------------
- ---------------- | ----------------
- ---------------- | ----------------
- ---------------- | ----------------

MY TASKS

- --
- --
- --
- --
- --
- --
- --
- --

BFAST	LUNCH	DINNER

SNACKS	EXERCISE

OUTFIT

IMPORTANT NOTE

THU

MY TASKS

....
....
....
....
....
....
....
....
....

BFAST	LUNCH	DINNER

SNACKS	EXERCISE

OUTFIT

IMPORTANT NOTE

THINGS I SHOULD TAKE NOTES OF

....
....
....
....
....
....
....
....

FRI

MY TASKS

....
....
....
....
....
....
....
....

BFAST	LUNCH	DINNER

SNACKS	EXERCISE

OUTFIT

IMPORTANT NOTE

....
....
....
....
....
....
....

SAT

MY TASKS

....
....
....
....

BFAST	LUNCH	DINNER

OUTFIT

SUN

MY TASKS

....
....
....
....

BFAST	LUNCH	DINNER

OUTFIT

WEEKLY REVIEW

NO. OF GOALS ACHIEVED?..............
LESSONS LEARNED?

....
....
....

HIGHLIGHTS THIS WEEK?

....
....

AM I HAPPY WITH THE RESULT?

DATE	WEEK

MY GOALS

DONE

- .... ☐
- .... ☐
- .... ☐
- .... ☐
- .... ☐
- .... ☐
- .... ☐
- .... ☐

MY TASKS

- ....
- ....
- ....
- ....
- ....
- ....
- ....
- ....

BFAST	LUNCH	DINNER

SNACKS	EXERCISE

OUTFIT

IMPORTANT NOTE

MY STRATEGIES

- ....
- ....
- ....
- ....
- ....
- ....
- ....
- ....

MY TASKS

- ....
- ....
- ....
- ....
- ....
- ....
- ....
- ....

BFAST	LUNCH	DINNER

SNACKS	EXERCISE

OUTFIT

IMPORTANT NOTE

SHOPPING LIST

MY TASKS

- ....
- ....
- ....
- ....
- ....
- ....
- ....
- ....

BFAST	LUNCH	DINNER

SNACKS	EXERCISE

OUTFIT

IMPORTANT NOTE

THU

MY TASKS

....
....
....
....
....
....
....

BFAST LUNCH DINNER

SNACKS   EXERCISE

OUTFIT

IMPORTANT NOTE

THINGS I SHOULD TAKE NOTES OF

....
....
....
....
....
....
....
....

FRI

MY TASKS

....
....
....
....
....
....
....

BFAST LUNCH DINNER

SNACKS   EXERCISE

OUTFIT

IMPORTANT NOTE

....
....
....
....
....

SAT

MY TASKS

....
....
....
....

BFAST LUNCH DINNER

OUTFIT

SUN

MY TASKS

....
....
....
....

BFAST LUNCH DINNER

OUTFIT

WEEKLY REVIEW

NO. OF GOALS ACHIEVED?.............
LESSONS LEARNED?
....
....
....

HIGHLIGHTS THIS WEEK?
....
....

AM I HAPPY WITH THE RESULT?

DATE	WEEK

MY GOALS

	DONE
....	☐
....	☐
....	☐
....	☐
....	☐
....	☐
....	☐
....	☐

MY STRATEGIES

....

....

....

....

....

....

....

....

SHOPPING LIST	
....	....
....	....
....	....
....	....
....	....
....	....
....	....

MY TASKS

....

....

....

....

....

....

....

BFAST	LUNCH	DINNER

SNACKS	EXERCISE

OUTFIT

IMPORTANT NOTE

MY TASKS

....

....

....

....

....

....

....

BFAST	LUNCH	DINNER

SNACKS	EXERCISE

OUTFIT

IMPORTANT NOTE

MY TASKS

....

....

....

....

....

....

....

BFAST	LUNCH	DINNER

SNACKS	EXERCISE

OUTFIT

IMPORTANT NOTE

MY TASKS — THU

....
....
....
....
....
....
....

BFAST	LUNCH	DINNER

SNACKS	EXERCISE

OUTFIT

IMPORTANT NOTE

THINGS I SHOULD TAKE NOTES OF

....
....
....
....
....
....
....

MY TASKS — FRI

....
....
....
....
....
....
....

BFAST	LUNCH	DINNER

SNACKS	EXERCISE

OUTFIT

IMPORTANT NOTE

....
....
....
....
....
....

MY TASKS — SAT

....
....
....

BFAST	LUNCH	DINNER

OUTFIT

MY TASKS — SUN

....
....
....

BFAST	LUNCH	DINNER

OUTFIT

WEEKLY REVIEW

NO. OF GOALS ACHIEVED?..........
LESSONS LEARNED?

....
....
....

HIGHLIGHTS THIS WEEK?

....
....
....

AM I HAPPY WITH THE RESULT?

DATE	WEEK

MY GOALS   DONE

- .... ☐
- .... ☐
- .... ☐
- .... ☐
- .... ☐
- .... ☐
- .... ☐
- .... ☐

MY TASKS

- ....
- ....
- ....
- ....
- ....
- ....
- ....
- ....

BFAST	LUNCH	DINNER

SNACKS	EXERCISE

OUTFIT

IMPORTANT NOTE

MY STRATEGIES

- ....
- ....
- ....
- ....
- ....
- ....
- ....
- ....

MY TASKS

- ....
- ....
- ....
- ....
- ....
- ....
- ....
- ....

BFAST	LUNCH	DINNER

SNACKS	EXERCISE

OUTFIT

IMPORTANT NOTE

SHOPPING LIST

....	....
....	....
....	....
....	....
....	....
....	....
....	....

MY TASKS

- ....
- ....
- ....
- ....
- ....
- ....
- ....

BFAST	LUNCH	DINNER

SNACKS	EXERCISE

OUTFIT

IMPORTANT NOTE

MY TASKS

THU

·····
·····
·····
·····
·····
·····
·····

BFAST	LUNCH	DINNER

SNACKS	EXERCISE

OUTFIT

IMPORTANT NOTE

THINGS I SHOULD TAKE NOTES OF

·····
·····
·····
·····
·····
·····
·····
·····
·····

MY TASKS

FRI

·····
·····
·····
·····
·····
·····
·····

BFAST	LUNCH	DINNER

SNACKS	EXERCISE

OUTFIT

IMPORTANT NOTE

·····
·····
·····
·····
·····
·····
·····
·····

MY TASKS

SAT

·····
·····
·····
·····

BFAST	LUNCH	DINNER

OUTFIT

MY TASKS

SUN

·····
·····
·····
·····

BFAST	LUNCH	DINNER

OUTFIT

WEEKLY REVIEW

NO. OF GOALS ACHIEVED?·····
LESSONS LEARNED?

·····
·····
·····

HIGHLIGHTS THIS WEEK?

·····
·····

AM I HAPPY WITH THE RESULT?

DATE	WEEK

MY GOALS / DONE

- .... ☐
- .... ☐
- .... ☐
- .... ☐
- .... ☐
- .... ☐
- .... ☐
- .... ☐

MY STRATEGIES

- ....
- ....
- ....
- ....
- ....
- ....
- ....
- ....

SHOPPING LIST

....	
....	
....	
....	
....	
....	
....	
....	

MY TASKS

- ....
- ....
- ....
- ....
- ....
- ....
- ....

BFAST	LUNCH	DINNER

SNACKS	EXERCISE

OUTFIT

IMPORTANT NOTE

MY TASKS

- ....
- ....
- ....
- ....
- ....
- ....

BFAST	LUNCH	DINNER

SNACKS	EXERCISE

OUTFIT

IMPORTANT NOTE

MY TASKS

- ....
- ....
- ....
- ....
- ....
- ....

BFAST	LUNCH	DINNER

SNACKS	EXERCISE

OUTFIT

IMPORTANT NOTE

THU

MY TASKS

BFAST	LUNCH	DINNER

SNACKS	EXERCISE

OUTFIT

IMPORTANT NOTE

THINGS I SHOULD TAKE NOTES OF

FRI

MY TASKS

BFAST	LUNCH	DINNER

SNACKS	EXERCISE

OUTFIT

IMPORTANT NOTE

SAT

MY TASKS

BFAST	LUNCH	DINNER

OUTFIT

SUN

MY TASKS

BFAST	LUNCH	DINNER

OUTFIT

WEEKLY REVIEW

NO. OF GOALS ACHIEVED?..............
LESSONS LEARNED?

HIGHLIGHTS THIS WEEK?

AM I HAPPY WITH THE RESULT?

DATE	WEEK

MY GOALS   DONE

- .... ☐
- .... ☐
- .... ☐
- .... ☐
- .... ☐
- .... ☐
- .... ☐
- .... ☐

MY STRATEGIES

- ....
- ....
- ....
- ....
- ....
- ....
- ....
- ....

SHOPPING LIST

MY TASKS

- ....
- ....
- ....
- ....
- ....
- ....
- ....

MON

BFAST	LUNCH	DINNER

SNACKS	EXERCISE

OUTFIT

IMPORTANT NOTE

MY TASKS

- ....
- ....
- ....
- ....
- ....
- ....
- ....

TUE

BFAST	LUNCH	DINNER

SNACKS	EXERCISE

OUTFIT

IMPORTANT NOTE

MY TASKS

- ....
- ....
- ....
- ....
- ....
- ....
- ....

WED

BFAST	LUNCH	DINNER

SNACKS	EXERCISE

OUTFIT

IMPORTANT NOTE

THU

MY TASKS

....
....
....
....
....
....
....
....

BFAST	LUNCH	DINNER

SNACKS	EXERCISE

OUTFIT

IMPORTANT NOTE

THINGS I SHOULD TAKE NOTES OF

....
....
....
....
....
....
....
....
....
....

FRI

MY TASKS

....
....
....
....
....
....
....
....

BFAST	LUNCH	DINNER

SNACKS	EXERCISE

OUTFIT

IMPORTANT NOTE

....
....
....
....
....
....
....
....

SAT

MY TASKS

....
....
....
....
....

BFAST	LUNCH	DINNER

OUTFIT

SUN

MY TASKS

....
....
....
....
....

BFAST	LUNCH	DINNER

OUTFIT

WEEKLY REVIEW

NO. OF GOALS ACHIEVED?...............
LESSONS LEARNED?
....
....
....

HIGHLIGHTS THIS WEEK?
....
....
....

AM I HAPPY WITH THE RESULT?

DATE	WEEK

MY GOALS   DONE

- .... ☐
- .... ☐
- .... ☐
- .... ☐
- .... ☐
- .... ☐
- .... ☐
- .... ☐

MY TASKS

- ....
- ....
- ....
- ....
- ....
- ....
- ....
- ....

BFAST	LUNCH	DINNER

SNACKS	EXERCISE

OUTFIT

IMPORTANT NOTE

MY STRATEGIES

- ....
- ....
- ....
- ....
- ....
- ....
- ....
- ....

MY TASKS

- ....
- ....
- ....
- ....
- ....
- ....
- ....
- ....

BFAST	LUNCH	DINNER

SNACKS	EXERCISE

OUTFIT

IMPORTANT NOTE

SHOPPING LIST

- ....
- ....
- ....
- ....
- ....
- ....
- ....
- ....

MY TASKS

- ....
- ....
- ....
- ....
- ....
- ....
- ....
- ....

BFAST	LUNCH	DINNER

SNACKS	EXERCISE

OUTFIT

IMPORTANT NOTE

MY TASKS

THU

....
....
....
....
....
....

BFAST	LUNCH	DINNER

SNACKS	EXERCISE

OUTFIT

IMPORTANT NOTE

THINGS I SHOULD TAKE NOTES OF

....
....
....
....
....
....
....
....
....

MY TASKS

FRI

....
....
....
....
....
....

BFAST	LUNCH	DINNER

SNACKS	EXERCISE

OUTFIT

IMPORTANT NOTE

....
....
....
....
....
....
....

MY TASKS

SAT

....
....
....
....

BFAST	LUNCH	DINNER

OUTFIT

MY TASKS

SUN

....
....
....
....

BFAST	LUNCH	DINNER

OUTFIT

WEEKLY REVIEW

NO. OF GOALS ACHIEVED?..............
LESSONS LEARNED?

....
....
....

HIGHLIGHTS THIS WEEK?

....
....
....

AM I HAPPY WITH THE RESULT?

DATE	WEEK

MY GOALS | DONE

----------------------------------- ☐
----------------------------------- ☐
----------------------------------- ☐
----------------------------------- ☐
----------------------------------- ☐
----------------------------------- ☐
----------------------------------- ☐
----------------------------------- ☐
----------------------------------- ☐

MY TASKS

BFAST	LUNCH	DINNER

SNACKS	EXERCISE

OUTFIT

IMPORTANT NOTE

MY STRATEGIES

MY TASKS

BFAST	LUNCH	DINNER

SNACKS	EXERCISE

OUTFIT

IMPORTANT NOTE

SHOPPING LIST

MY TASKS

BFAST	LUNCH	DINNER

SNACKS	EXERCISE

OUTFIT

IMPORTANT NOTE

THU

MY TASKS

- ....
- ....
- ....
- ....
- ....
- ....
- ....

BFAST	LUNCH	DINNER

SNACKS	EXERCISE

OUTFIT

IMPORTANT NOTE

THINGS I SHOULD TAKE NOTES OF

- ....
- ....
- ....
- ....
- ....
- ....
- ....
- ....
- ....
- ....

FRI

MY TASKS

- ....
- ....
- ....
- ....
- ....
- ....
- ....

BFAST	LUNCH	DINNER

SNACKS	EXERCISE

OUTFIT

IMPORTANT NOTE

- ....
- ....
- ....
- ....
- ....
- ....
- ....
- ....

SAT

MY TASKS

- ....
- ....
- ....
- ....

BFAST	LUNCH	DINNER

OUTFIT

SUN

MY TASKS

- ....
- ....
- ....
- ....

BFAST	LUNCH	DINNER

OUTFIT

WEEKLY REVIEW

NO. OF GOALS ACHIEVED? ....
LESSONS LEARNED?

- ....
- ....
- ....

HIGHLIGHTS THIS WEEK?

- ....
- ....

AM I HAPPY WITH THE RESULT?

DATE	WEEK

MY GOALS | DONE

.... ☐
.... ☐
.... ☐
.... ☐
.... ☐
.... ☐
.... ☐
.... ☐

MY STRATEGIES

....
....
....
....
....
....
....
....

SHOPPING LIST

....	....
....	....
....	....
....	....
....	....
....	....
....	....

MY TASKS

....
....
....
....
....
....

BFAST	LUNCH	DINNER

SNACKS	EXERCISE

OUTFIT

IMPORTANT NOTE

MY TASKS

....
....
....
....
....
....

BFAST	LUNCH	DINNER

SNACKS	EXERCISE

OUTFIT

IMPORTANT NOTE

MY TASKS

....
....
....
....
....
....

BFAST	LUNCH	DINNER

SNACKS	EXERCISE

OUTFIT

IMPORTANT NOTE

MY TASKS

THU

....
....
....
....
....
....

BFAST	LUNCH	DINNER

SNACKS	EXERCISE

OUTFIT

IMPORTANT NOTE

THINGS I SHOULD TAKE NOTES OF

....
....
....
....
....
....
....

MY TASKS

FRI

....
....
....
....
....
....

BFAST	LUNCH	DINNER

SNACKS	EXERCISE

OUTFIT

IMPORTANT NOTE

....
....
....
....
....
....
....

MY TASKS

SAT

....
....
....
....

BFAST	LUNCH	DINNER

OUTFIT

MY TASKS

SUN

....
....
....
....

BFAST	LUNCH	DINNER

OUTFIT

WEEKLY REVIEW

NO. OF GOALS ACHIEVED?...............
LESSONS LEARNED?

....
....
....

HIGHLIGHTS THIS WEEK?

....
....
....

AM I HAPPY WITH THE RESULT?

DATE	WEEK

MY GOALS / DONE

- .... ☐
- .... ☐
- .... ☐
- .... ☐
- .... ☐
- .... ☐
- .... ☐
- .... ☐
- .... ☐

MY TASKS

- ....
- ....
- ....
- ....
- ....
- ....
- ....

BFAST	LUNCH	DINNER

SNACKS	EXERCISE

OUTFIT

IMPORTANT NOTE

MY STRATEGIES

- ....
- ....
- ....
- ....
- ....
- ....
- ....
- ....

MY TASKS

- ....
- ....
- ....
- ....
- ....
- ....
- ....

BFAST	LUNCH	DINNER

SNACKS	EXERCISE

OUTFIT

IMPORTANT NOTE

SHOPPING LIST

- .... | ....
- .... | ....
- .... | ....
- .... | ....
- .... | ....
- .... | ....
- .... | ....

MY TASKS

- ....
- ....
- ....
- ....
- ....
- ....
- ....

BFAST	LUNCH	DINNER

SNACKS	EXERCISE

OUTFIT

IMPORTANT NOTE

THU

MY TASKS
....
....
....
....
....
....

BFAST	LUNCH	DINNER

SNACKS	EXERCISE

OUTFIT

IMPORTANT NOTE

THINGS I SHOULD TAKE NOTES OF
....
....
....
....
....
....
....
....

FRI

MY TASKS
....
....
....
....
....
....

BFAST	LUNCH	DINNER

SNACKS	EXERCISE

OUTFIT

IMPORTANT NOTE

....
....
....
....
....
....
....

SAT

MY TASKS
....
....
....
....

BFAST	LUNCH	DINNER

OUTFIT

SUN

MY TASKS
....
....
....
....

BFAST	LUNCH	DINNER

OUTFIT

WEEKLY REVIEW
NO. OF GOALS ACHIEVED?................
LESSONS LEARNED?
....
....
....

HIGHLIGHTS THIS WEEK?
....
....
....

AM I HAPPY WITH THE RESULT?

DATE	WEEK

MY GOALS

DONE

- .... ☐
- .... ☐
- .... ☐
- .... ☐
- .... ☐
- .... ☐
- .... ☐
- .... ☐
- .... ☐

MY TASKS

- ....
- ....
- ....
- ....
- ....
- ....
- ....
- ....
- ....

BFAST	LUNCH	DINNER

SNACKS	EXERCISE

OUTFIT

IMPORTANT NOTE

MY STRATEGIES

- ....
- ....
- ....
- ....
- ....
- ....
- ....
- ....

MY TASKS

- ....
- ....
- ....
- ....
- ....
- ....
- ....
- ....

BFAST	LUNCH	DINNER

SNACKS	EXERCISE

OUTFIT

IMPORTANT NOTE

SHOPPING LIST

MY TASKS

- ....
- ....
- ....
- ....
- ....
- ....
- ....
- ....

BFAST	LUNCH	DINNER

SNACKS	EXERCISE

OUTFIT

IMPORTANT NOTE

THU

MY TASKS

....
....
....
....
....
....

BFAST	LUNCH	DINNER

SNACKS	EXERCISE

OUTFIT

IMPORTANT NOTE

THINGS I SHOULD TAKE NOTES OF

....
....
....
....
....
....
....

FRI

MY TASKS

....
....
....
....
....
....

BFAST	LUNCH	DINNER

SNACKS	EXERCISE

OUTFIT

IMPORTANT NOTE

....
....
....
....
....

SAT

MY TASKS

....
....
....
....

BFAST	LUNCH	DINNER

OUTFIT

SUN

MY TASKS

....
....
....
....

BFAST	LUNCH	DINNER

OUTFIT

WEEKLY REVIEW

NO. OF GOALS ACHIEVED?...............
LESSONS LEARNED?

....
....
....

HIGHLIGHTS THIS WEEK?

....
....

AM I HAPPY WITH THE RESULT?

DATE	WEEK

MY GOALS   DONE

- .... ☐
- .... ☐
- .... ☐
- .... ☐
- .... ☐
- .... ☐
- .... ☐
- .... ☐
- .... ☐

MY STRATEGIES

- ....
- ....
- ....
- ....
- ....
- ....
- ....
- ....
- ....

SHOPPING LIST

MY TASKS

- ....
- ....
- ....
- ....
- ....
- ....
- ....

BFAST	LUNCH	DINNER

SNACKS	EXERCISE

OUTFIT

IMPORTANT NOTE

MY TASKS

- ....
- ....
- ....
- ....
- ....
- ....
- ....

BFAST	LUNCH	DINNER

SNACKS	EXERCISE

OUTFIT

IMPORTANT NOTE

MY TASKS

- ....
- ....
- ....
- ....
- ....
- ....
- ....

BFAST	LUNCH	DINNER

SNACKS	EXERCISE

OUTFIT

IMPORTANT NOTE

MY TASKS

THU

....
....
....
....
....
....

BFAST	LUNCH	DINNER

SNACKS	EXERCISE

OUTFIT

IMPORTANT NOTE

THINGS I SHOULD TAKE NOTES OF

....
....
....
....
....
....
....
....

MY TASKS

FRI

....
....
....
....
....
....

BFAST	LUNCH	DINNER

SNACKS	EXERCISE

OUTFIT

IMPORTANT NOTE

....
....
....
....
....
....
....

MY TASKS

SAT

....
....
....
....

BFAST	LUNCH	DINNER

OUTFIT

MY TASKS

SUN

....
....
....
....

BFAST	LUNCH	DINNER

OUTFIT

WEEKLY REVIEW

NO. OF GOALS ACHIEVED?...............
LESSONS LEARNED?

....
....
....

HIGHLIGHTS THIS WEEK?

....
....
....

AM I HAPPY WITH THE RESULT?

DATE	WEEK

MY GOALS　　　　　DONE

- .... ☐
- .... ☐
- .... ☐
- .... ☐
- .... ☐
- .... ☐
- .... ☐
- .... ☐
- .... ☐

MY TASKS

- ....
- ....
- ....
- ....
- ....
- ....
- ....
- ....

BFAST	LUNCH	DINNER

SNACKS	EXERCISE

OUTFIT

IMPORTANT NOTE

MY STRATEGIES

- ....
- ....
- ....
- ....
- ....
- ....
- ....
- ....

MY TASKS

- ....
- ....
- ....
- ....
- ....
- ....
- ....

BFAST	LUNCH	DINNER

SNACKS	EXERCISE

OUTFIT

IMPORTANT NOTE

SHOPPING LIST

....	....
....	....
....	....
....	....
....	....
....	....
....	....

MY TASKS

- ....
- ....
- ....
- ....
- ....
- ....
- ....

BFAST	LUNCH	DINNER

SNACKS	EXERCISE

OUTFIT

IMPORTANT NOTE

MY TASKS (THU)

	BFAST	LUNCH	DINNER

SNACKS	EXERCISE

OUTFIT

IMPORTANT NOTE

THINGS I SHOULD TAKE NOTES OF

MY TASKS (FRI)

	BFAST	LUNCH	DINNER

SNACKS	EXERCISE

OUTFIT

IMPORTANT NOTE

MY TASKS (SAT)

BFAST	LUNCH	DINNER

OUTFIT

MY TASKS (SUN)

BFAST	LUNCH	DINNER

OUTFIT

WEEKLY REVIEW

NO. OF GOALS ACHIEVED?
LESSONS LEARNED?

HIGHLIGHTS THIS WEEK?

AM I HAPPY WITH THE RESULT?

DATE	WEEK

MY GOALS   DONE

- .... ☐
- .... ☐
- .... ☐
- .... ☐
- .... ☐
- .... ☐
- .... ☐
- .... ☐
- .... ☐

MY STRATEGIES

- ....
- ....
- ....
- ....
- ....
- ....
- ....
- ....

SHOPPING LIST

- ....
- ....
- ....
- ....
- ....
- ....
- ....
- ....

MY TASKS

- ....
- ....
- ....
- ....
- ....
- ....
- ....
- ....

MY TASKS

- ....
- ....
- ....
- ....
- ....
- ....
- ....

MY TASKS

- ....
- ....
- ....
- ....
- ....
- ....
- ....

BFAST	LUNCH	DINNER

SNACKS	EXERCISE

OUTFIT

IMPORTANT NOTE

BFAST	LUNCH	DINNER

SNACKS	EXERCISE

OUTFIT

IMPORTANT NOTE

BFAST	LUNCH	DINNER

SNACKS	EXERCISE

OUTFIT

IMPORTANT NOTE

THU

MY TASKS

- ....
- ....
- ....
- ....
- ....
- ....
- ....

BFAST	LUNCH	DINNER

SNACKS	EXERCISE

OUTFIT

IMPORTANT NOTE

THINGS I SHOULD TAKE NOTES OF

- ....
- ....
- ....
- ....
- ....
- ....
- ....
- ....
- ....
- ....
- ....
- ....
- ....
- ....
- ....
- ....
- ....
- ....
- ....

FRI

MY TASKS

- ....
- ....
- ....
- ....
- ....
- ....
- ....

BFAST	LUNCH	DINNER

SNACKS	EXERCISE

OUTFIT

IMPORTANT NOTE

SAT

MY TASKS

- ....
- ....
- ....
- ....
- ....

BFAST	LUNCH	DINNER

OUTFIT

SUN

MY TASKS

- ....
- ....
- ....
- ....
- ....

BFAST	LUNCH	DINNER

OUTFIT

WEEKLY REVIEW

NO. OF GOALS ACHIEVED?.............
LESSONS LEARNED?

- ....
- ....
- ....

HIGHLIGHTS THIS WEEK?

- ....
- ....
- ....

AM I HAPPY WITH THE RESULT?

DATE	WEEK

MY GOALS · DONE

.... ☐
.... ☐
.... ☐
.... ☐
.... ☐
.... ☐
.... ☐
.... ☐
.... ☐

MY STRATEGIES

....
....
....
....
....
....
....

SHOPPING LIST

....
....
....
....
....
....
....
....

MY TASKS

....
....
....
....
....
....
....
....

MY TASKS

....
....
....
....
....
....
....

MY TASKS

....
....
....
....
....
....
....

BFAST	LUNCH	DINNER

SNACKS	EXERCISE

OUTFIT

IMPORTANT NOTE

BFAST	LUNCH	DINNER

SNACKS	EXERCISE

OUTFIT

IMPORTANT NOTE

BFAST	LUNCH	DINNER

SNACKS	EXERCISE

OUTFIT

IMPORTANT NOTE

THU

MY TASKS

....
....
....
....
....
....
....

BFAST	LUNCH	DINNER

SNACKS	EXERCISE

OUTFIT

IMPORTANT NOTE

THINGS I SHOULD TAKE NOTES OF

....
....
....
....
....
....
....
....
....
....
....

FRI

MY TASKS

....
....
....
....
....
....
....

BFAST	LUNCH	DINNER

SNACKS	EXERCISE

OUTFIT

IMPORTANT NOTE

....
....
....
....
....
....
....
....

SAT

MY TASKS

....
....
....
....

BFAST	LUNCH	DINNER

OUTFIT

SUN

MY TASKS

....
....
....
....

BFAST	LUNCH	DINNER

OUTFIT

WEEKLY REVIEW

NO. OF GOALS ACHIEVED?.................
LESSONS LEARNED?

....
....
....

HIGHLIGHTS THIS WEEK?

....
....
....

AM I HAPPY WITH THE RESULT?

DATE	WEEK

MY GOALS

DONE

.... ☐
.... ☐
.... ☐
.... ☐
.... ☐
.... ☐
.... ☐
.... ☐
.... ☐

MY STRATEGIES

....
....
....
....
....
....
....
....

SHOPPING LIST	
....	
....	
....	
....	
....	
....	
....	
....	

MY TASKS

....
....
....
....
....
....
....
....

BFAST	LUNCH	DINNER

SNACKS	EXERCISE

OUTFIT

IMPORTANT NOTE

MY TASKS

....
....
....
....
....
....
....
....

BFAST	LUNCH	DINNER

SNACKS	EXERCISE

OUTFIT

IMPORTANT NOTE

MY TASKS

....
....
....
....
....
....
....
....

BFAST	LUNCH	DINNER

SNACKS	EXERCISE

OUTFIT

IMPORTANT NOTE

THU

MY TASKS

....

....

....

....

....

....

....

BFAST	LUNCH	DINNER

SNACKS	EXERCISE

OUTFIT

IMPORTANT NOTE

THINGS I SHOULD TAKE NOTES OF

....

....

....

....

....

....

....

....

....

FRI

MY TASKS

....

....

....

....

....

....

....

BFAST	LUNCH	DINNER

SNACKS	EXERCISE

OUTFIT

IMPORTANT NOTE

....

....

....

....

....

....

....

....

SAT

MY TASKS

....

....

....

....

....

BFAST	LUNCH	DINNER

OUTFIT

SUN

MY TASKS

....

....

....

....

....

BFAST	LUNCH	DINNER

OUTFIT

WEEKLY REVIEW

NO. OF GOALS ACHIEVED? ....

LESSONS LEARNED?

....

....

....

HIGHLIGHTS THIS WEEK?

....

....

....

AM I HAPPY WITH THE RESULT?

DATE	WEEK

MY GOALS

DONE

.... ☐
.... ☐
.... ☐
.... ☐
.... ☐
.... ☐
.... ☐
.... ☐
.... ☐

MY STRATEGIES

....
....
....
....
....
....
....
....

SHOPPING LIST	

MY TASKS

....
....
....
....
....
....
....
....

MY TASKS

....
....
....
....
....
....
....
....

MY TASKS

....
....
....
....
....
....
....

BFAST	LUNCH	DINNER

SNACKS	EXERCISE

OUTFIT

IMPORTANT NOTE

BFAST	LUNCH	DINNER

SNACKS	EXERCISE

OUTFIT

IMPORTANT NOTE

BFAST	LUNCH	DINNER

SNACKS	EXERCISE

OUTFIT

IMPORTANT NOTE

THU

MY TASKS

....
....
....
....
....
....

BFAST	LUNCH	DINNER

SNACKS	EXERCISE

OUTFIT

IMPORTANT NOTE

THINGS I SHOULD TAKE NOTES OF

....
....
....
....
....
....
....

FRI

MY TASKS

....
....
....
....
....
....

BFAST	LUNCH	DINNER

SNACKS	EXERCISE

OUTFIT

IMPORTANT NOTE

....
....
....
....
....

SAT

MY TASKS

....
....
....
....

BFAST	LUNCH	DINNER

OUTFIT

SUN

MY TASKS

....
....
....
....

BFAST	LUNCH	DINNER

OUTFIT

WEEKLY REVIEW

NO. OF GOALS ACHIEVED?..........
LESSONS LEARNED?
....
....
....

HIGHLIGHTS THIS WEEK?
....
....

AM I HAPPY WITH THE RESULT?

DATE	WEEK

MY GOALS

	DONE
....	☐
....	☐
....	☐
....	☐
....	☐
....	☐
....	☐
....	☐

MY STRATEGIES

....

....

....

....

....

....

....

....

SHOPPING LIST

....	
....	
....	
....	
....	
....	
....	
....	

MY TASKS

....

....

....

....

....

....

BFAST	LUNCH	DINNER

SNACKS	EXERCISE

OUTFIT

IMPORTANT NOTE

MY TASKS

....

....

....

....

....

....

BFAST	LUNCH	DINNER

SNACKS	EXERCISE

OUTFIT

IMPORTANT NOTE

MY TASKS

....

....

....

....

....

....

BFAST	LUNCH	DINNER

SNACKS	EXERCISE

OUTFIT

IMPORTANT NOTE

THU

MY TASKS

- ....
- ....
- ....
- ....
- ....
- ....
- ....
- ....

BFAST	LUNCH	DINNER

SNACKS	EXERCISE

OUTFIT

IMPORTANT NOTE

THINGS I SHOULD TAKE NOTES OF

- ....
- ....
- ....
- ....
- ....
- ....
- ....

FRI

MY TASKS

- ....
- ....
- ....
- ....
- ....
- ....

BFAST	LUNCH	DINNER

SNACKS	EXERCISE

OUTFIT

IMPORTANT NOTE

- ....
- ....
- ....
- ....
- ....
- ....
- ....

SAT

MY TASKS

- ....
- ....
- ....
- ....
- ....

BFAST	LUNCH	DINNER

OUTFIT

SUN

MY TASKS

- ....
- ....
- ....
- ....
- ....

BFAST	LUNCH	DINNER

OUTFIT

WEEKLY REVIEW

NO. OF GOALS ACHIEVED?.................
LESSONS LEARNED?

- ....
- ....
- ....

HIGHLIGHTS THIS WEEK?

- ....
- ....

AM I HAPPY WITH THE RESULT?

DATE	WEEK

MY GOALS — DONE

- .... ☐
- .... ☐
- .... ☐
- .... ☐
- .... ☐
- .... ☐
- .... ☐
- .... ☐

MY TASKS

- ....
- ....
- ....
- ....
- ....
- ....

BFAST	LUNCH	DINNER

SNACKS	EXERCISE

OUTFIT

IMPORTANT NOTE

MY STRATEGIES

- ....
- ....
- ....
- ....
- ....
- ....
- ....

MY TASKS

- ....
- ....
- ....
- ....
- ....
- ....

BFAST	LUNCH	DINNER

SNACKS	EXERCISE

OUTFIT

IMPORTANT NOTE

SHOPPING LIST

- .... | ....
- .... | ....
- .... | ....
- .... | ....
- .... | ....
- .... | ....
- .... | ....

MY TASKS

- ....
- ....
- ....
- ....
- ....
- ....

BFAST	LUNCH	DINNER

SNACKS	EXERCISE

OUTFIT

IMPORTANT NOTE

THU

MY TASKS

....
....
....
....
....
....
....
....

BFAST	LUNCH	DINNER

SNACKS	EXERCISE

OUTFIT

IMPORTANT NOTE

THINGS I SHOULD TAKE NOTES OF

....
....
....
....
....
....
....
....
....
....
....

FRI

MY TASKS

....
....
....
....
....
....
....
....

BFAST	LUNCH	DINNER

SNACKS	EXERCISE

OUTFIT

IMPORTANT NOTE

SAT

MY TASKS

....
....
....
....

BFAST	LUNCH	DINNER

OUTFIT

SUN

MY TASKS

....
....
....
....

BFAST	LUNCH	DINNER

OUTFIT

WEEKLY REVIEW

NO. OF GOALS ACHIEVED?..............
LESSONS LEARNED?

....
....
....

HIGHLIGHTS THIS WEEK?

....
....

AM I HAPPY WITH THE RESULT?

DATE	WEEK

MY GOALS — DONE

- .... ☐
- .... ☐
- .... ☐
- .... ☐
- .... ☐
- .... ☐
- .... ☐
- .... ☐
- .... ☐

MY TASKS

- ....
- ....
- ....
- ....
- ....
- ....
- ....

BFAST	LUNCH	DINNER

SNACKS	EXERCISE

OUTFIT

IMPORTANT NOTE

MY STRATEGIES

- ....
- ....
- ....
- ....
- ....
- ....
- ....
- ....

MY TASKS

- ....
- ....
- ....
- ....
- ....
- ....
- ....

BFAST	LUNCH	DINNER

SNACKS	EXERCISE

OUTFIT

IMPORTANT NOTE

SHOPPING LIST

MY TASKS

- ....
- ....
- ....
- ....
- ....
- ....
- ....

BFAST	LUNCH	DINNER

SNACKS	EXERCISE

OUTFIT

IMPORTANT NOTE

MY TASKS

THU

....
....
....
....
....
....
....

BFAST	LUNCH	DINNER

SNACKS	EXERCISE

OUTFIT

IMPORTANT NOTE

THINGS I SHOULD TAKE NOTES OF

....
....
....
....
....
....
....
....
....
....

MY TASKS

FRI

....
....
....
....
....
....
....

BFAST	LUNCH	DINNER

SNACKS	EXERCISE

OUTFIT

IMPORTANT NOTE

....
....
....
....
....
....
....

MY TASKS

SAT

....
....
....
....

BFAST	LUNCH	DINNER

OUTFIT

MY TASKS

SUN

....
....
....
....

BFAST	LUNCH	DINNER

OUTFIT

WEEKLY REVIEW

NO. OF GOALS ACHIEVED?...............
LESSONS LEARNED?
....
....
....

HIGHLIGHTS THIS WEEK?
....
....

AM I HAPPY WITH THE RESULT?

DATE	WEEK

MY GOALS

DONE

.... ☐
.... ☐
.... ☐
.... ☐
.... ☐
.... ☐
.... ☐
.... ☐
.... ☐

MY TASKS

....
....
....
....
....
....
....
....
....

BFAST	LUNCH	DINNER

SNACKS	EXERCISE

OUTFIT

IMPORTANT NOTE

MY STRATEGIES

....
....
....
....
....
....
....
....

MY TASKS

....
....
....
....
....
....
....
....

BFAST	LUNCH	DINNER

SNACKS	EXERCISE

OUTFIT

IMPORTANT NOTE

SHOPPING LIST

....
....
....
....
....
....
....
....

MY TASKS

....
....
....
....
....
....
....
....

BFAST	LUNCH	DINNER

SNACKS	EXERCISE

OUTFIT

IMPORTANT NOTE

MY TASKS

THU

....
....
....
....
....
....
....

BFAST	LUNCH	DINNER

SNACKS	EXERCISE

OUTFIT

IMPORTANT NOTE

THINGS I SHOULD TAKE NOTES OF

....
....
....
....
....
....
....
....

MY TASKS

FRI

....
....
....
....
....
....
....

BFAST	LUNCH	DINNER

SNACKS	EXERCISE

OUTFIT

IMPORTANT NOTE

....
....
....
....
....
....

MY TASKS

SAT

....
....
....
....

BFAST	LUNCH	DINNER

OUTFIT

MY TASKS

SUN

....
....
....
....

BFAST	LUNCH	DINNER

OUTFIT

WEEKLY REVIEW

NO. OF GOALS ACHIEVED?............
LESSONS LEARNED?

....
....
....

HIGHLIGHTS THIS WEEK?

....
....
....

AM I HAPPY WITH THE RESULT?

DATE	WEEK

MY GOALS | DONE

.... ☐
.... ☐
.... ☐
.... ☐
.... ☐
.... ☐
.... ☐
.... ☐

MY TASKS

....
....
....
....
....
....
....
....

BFAST	LUNCH	DINNER

SNACKS	EXERCISE

OUTFIT

IMPORTANT NOTE

MY STRATEGIES

....
....
....
....
....
....
....

MY TASKS

....
....
....
....
....
....
....

BFAST	LUNCH	DINNER

SNACKS	EXERCISE

OUTFIT

IMPORTANT NOTE

SHOPPING LIST

....
....
....
....
....
....
....

MY TASKS

....
....
....
....
....
....
....

BFAST	LUNCH	DINNER

SNACKS	EXERCISE

OUTFIT

IMPORTANT NOTE

MY TASKS (THU)

BFAST	LUNCH	DINNER

SNACKS	EXERCISE

OUTFIT

IMPORTANT NOTE

THINGS I SHOULD TAKE NOTES OF

MY TASKS (FRI)

BFAST	LUNCH	DINNER

SNACKS	EXERCISE

OUTFIT

IMPORTANT NOTE

MY TASKS (SAT)

BFAST	LUNCH	DINNER

OUTFIT

MY TASKS (SUN)

BFAST	LUNCH	DINNER

OUTFIT

WEEKLY REVIEW

NO. OF GOALS ACHIEVED?

LESSONS LEARNED?

HIGHLIGHTS THIS WEEK?

AM I HAPPY WITH THE RESULT?

DATE	WEEK

MY GOALS   DONE

.... ☐
.... ☐
.... ☐
.... ☐
.... ☐
.... ☐
.... ☐
.... ☐
.... ☐

MY TASKS

....
....
....
....
....
....
....

BFAST	LUNCH	DINNER

SNACKS	EXERCISE

OUTFIT

IMPORTANT NOTE

MY STRATEGIES

MY TASKS

....
....
....
....
....
....
....

BFAST	LUNCH	DINNER

SNACKS	EXERCISE

OUTFIT

IMPORTANT NOTE

SHOPPING LIST	

MY TASKS

....
....
....
....
....
....
....

BFAST	LUNCH	DINNER

SNACKS	EXERCISE

OUTFIT

IMPORTANT NOTE

THU

MY TASKS

....
....
....
....
....
....
....
....
....

BFAST	LUNCH	DINNER

SNACKS	EXERCISE

OUTFIT

IMPORTANT NOTE

THINGS I SHOULD TAKE NOTES OF

....
....
....
....
....
....
....

FRI

MY TASKS

....
....
....
....
....
....
....
....

BFAST	LUNCH	DINNER

SNACKS	EXERCISE

OUTFIT

IMPORTANT NOTE

....
....
....
....
....
....
....
....

SAT

MY TASKS

....
....
....
....

BFAST	LUNCH	DINNER

OUTFIT

SUN

MY TASKS

....
....
....
....

BFAST	LUNCH	DINNER

OUTFIT

WEEKLY REVIEW

NO. OF GOALS ACHIEVED?................
LESSONS LEARNED?

....
....
....

HIGHLIGHTS THIS WEEK?

....
....
....

AM I HAPPY WITH THE RESULT?

DATE	WEEK

MY GOALS / DONE

- .... ☐
- .... ☐
- .... ☐
- .... ☐
- .... ☐
- .... ☐
- .... ☐
- .... ☐
- .... ☐

MY TASKS

- ....
- ....
- ....
- ....
- ....
- ....
- ....
- ....

BFAST	LUNCH	DINNER

SNACKS	EXERCISE

OUTFIT

IMPORTANT NOTE

MY STRATEGIES

- ....
- ....
- ....
- ....
- ....
- ....
- ....

MY TASKS

- ....
- ....
- ....
- ....
- ....
- ....
- ....

BFAST	LUNCH	DINNER

SNACKS	EXERCISE

OUTFIT

IMPORTANT NOTE

SHOPPING LIST

- ....
- ....
- ....
- ....
- ....
- ....

MY TASKS

- ....
- ....
- ....
- ....
- ....
- ....
- ....

BFAST	LUNCH	DINNER

SNACKS	EXERCISE

OUTFIT

IMPORTANT NOTE

MY TASKS

THU

BFAST	LUNCH	DINNER

SNACKS	EXERCISE

OUTFIT

IMPORTANT NOTE

THINGS I SHOULD TAKE NOTES OF

MY TASKS

FRI

BFAST	LUNCH	DINNER

SNACKS	EXERCISE

OUTFIT

IMPORTANT NOTE

MY TASKS

SAT

BFAST	LUNCH	DINNER

OUTFIT

MY TASKS

SUN

BFAST	LUNCH	DINNER

OUTFIT

WEEKLY REVIEW

NO. OF GOALS ACHIEVED?
LESSONS LEARNED?

HIGHLIGHTS THIS WEEK?

AM I HAPPY WITH THE RESULT?

DATE	WEEK

MY GOALS | DONE

.... ☐
.... ☐
.... ☐
.... ☐
.... ☐
.... ☐
.... ☐
.... ☐
.... ☐

MY TASKS

....
....
....
....
....
....
....

BFAST	LUNCH	DINNER

SNACKS	EXERCISE

OUTFIT

IMPORTANT NOTE

MY STRATEGIES

MY TASKS

BFAST	LUNCH	DINNER

SNACKS	EXERCISE

OUTFIT

IMPORTANT NOTE

SHOPPING LIST

MY TASKS

BFAST	LUNCH	DINNER

SNACKS	EXERCISE

OUTFIT

IMPORTANT NOTE

MY TASKS — THU

- ....
- ....
- ....
- ....
- ....
- ....
- ....

BFAST	LUNCH	DINNER

SNACKS	EXERCISE

OUTFIT

IMPORTANT NOTE

THINGS I SHOULD TAKE NOTES OF

- ....
- ....
- ....
- ....
- ....
- ....
- ....
- ....
- ....

MY TASKS — FRI

- ....
- ....
- ....
- ....
- ....
- ....
- ....

BFAST	LUNCH	DINNER

SNACKS	EXERCISE

OUTFIT

IMPORTANT NOTE

- ....
- ....
- ....
- ....
- ....

MY TASKS — SAT

- ....
- ....
- ....
- ....

BFAST	LUNCH	DINNER

OUTFIT

MY TASKS — SUN

- ....
- ....
- ....
- ....

BFAST	LUNCH	DINNER

OUTFIT

WEEKLY REVIEW

NO. OF GOALS ACHIEVED?..............
LESSONS LEARNED?

- ....
- ....
- ....

HIGHLIGHTS THIS WEEK?

- ....
- ....

AM I HAPPY WITH THE RESULT?

DATE	WEEK

MY GOALS | DONE

- .... ☐
- .... ☐
- .... ☐
- .... ☐
- .... ☐
- .... ☐
- .... ☐
- .... ☐

MY STRATEGIES

- ....
- ....
- ....
- ....
- ....
- ....
- ....

SHOPPING LIST

MY TASKS

- ....
- ....
- ....
- ....
- ....

MY TASKS

- ....
- ....
- ....
- ....
- ....
- ....

MY TASKS

BFAST	LUNCH	DINNER

SNACKS	EXERCISE

OUTFIT

IMPORTANT NOTE

BFAST	LUNCH	DINNER

SNACKS	EXERCISE

OUTFIT

IMPORTANT NOTE

BFAST	LUNCH	DINNER

SNACKS	EXERCISE

OUTFIT

IMPORTANT NOTE

THU

MY TASKS

....
....
....
....
....
....

BFAST	LUNCH	DINNER

SNACKS	EXERCISE

OUTFIT

IMPORTANT NOTE

THINGS I SHOULD TAKE NOTES OF

....
....
....
....
....
....
....

FRI

MY TASKS

....
....
....
....
....
....

BFAST	LUNCH	DINNER

SNACKS	EXERCISE

OUTFIT

IMPORTANT NOTE

....
....
....
....

SAT

MY TASKS

....
....
....
....

BFAST	LUNCH	DINNER

OUTFIT

SUN

MY TASKS

....
....
....
....

BFAST	LUNCH	DINNER

OUTFIT

WEEKLY REVIEW

NO. OF GOALS ACHIEVED?..............
LESSONS LEARNED?

....
....
....

HIGHLIGHTS THIS WEEK?

....
....

AM I HAPPY WITH THE RESULT?

DATE	WEEK

MY GOALS | DONE

- .... ☐
- .... ☐
- .... ☐
- .... ☐
- .... ☐
- .... ☐
- .... ☐
- .... ☐

MY TASKS

- ....
- ....
- ....
- ....
- ....

BFAST	LUNCH	DINNER

SNACKS	EXERCISE

OUTFIT

IMPORTANT NOTE

MY STRATEGIES

- ....
- ....
- ....
- ....
- ....
- ....
- ....
- ....

MY TASKS

- ....
- ....
- ....
- ....
- ....
- ....

BFAST	LUNCH	DINNER

SNACKS	EXERCISE

OUTFIT

IMPORTANT NOTE

SHOPPING LIST

- ....
- ....
- ....
- ....
- ....
- ....
- ....

MY TASKS

- ....
- ....
- ....
- ....
- ....
- ....

BFAST	LUNCH	DINNER

SNACKS	EXERCISE

OUTFIT

IMPORTANT NOTE

THU

MY TASKS

....
....
....
....
....
....
....

BFAST	LUNCH	DINNER

SNACKS	EXERCISE

OUTFIT

IMPORTANT NOTE

THINGS I SHOULD TAKE NOTES OF

....
....
....
....
....
....
....
....

FRI

MY TASKS

....
....
....
....
....
....
....

BFAST	LUNCH	DINNER

SNACKS	EXERCISE

OUTFIT

IMPORTANT NOTE

....
....
....
....
....
....

SAT

MY TASKS

....
....
....
....

BFAST	LUNCH	DINNER

OUTFIT

SUN

MY TASKS

....
....
....
....

BFAST	LUNCH	DINNER

OUTFIT

WEEKLY REVIEW

NO. OF GOALS ACHIEVED?.................
LESSONS LEARNED?

....
....
....

HIGHLIGHTS THIS WEEK?

....
....

AM I HAPPY WITH THE RESULT?

DATE	WEEK

MY GOALS — DONE

- .... ☐
- .... ☐
- .... ☐
- .... ☐
- .... ☐
- .... ☐
- .... ☐
- .... ☐

MY STRATEGIES

- ....
- ....
- ....
- ....
- ....
- ....
- ....
- ....

SHOPPING LIST

....	....
....	....
....	....
....	....
....	....
....	....
....	....
....	....

MY TASKS

- ....
- ....
- ....
- ....
- ....
- ....
- ....
- ....

BFAST	LUNCH	DINNER

SNACKS	EXERCISE

OUTFIT

IMPORTANT NOTE

MY TASKS

- ....
- ....
- ....
- ....
- ....
- ....
- ....
- ....

BFAST	LUNCH	DINNER

SNACKS	EXERCISE

OUTFIT

IMPORTANT NOTE

MY TASKS

- ....
- ....
- ....
- ....
- ....
- ....
- ....
- ....

BFAST	LUNCH	DINNER

SNACKS	EXERCISE

OUTFIT

IMPORTANT NOTE

THU

MY TASKS

....
....
....
....
....
....
....

BFAST	LUNCH	DINNER

SNACKS	EXERCISE

OUTFIT

IMPORTANT NOTE

THINGS I SHOULD TAKE NOTES OF

....
....
....
....
....
....
....
....
....
....
....
....
....
....
....
....
....
....
....

FRI

MY TASKS

....
....
....
....
....
....
....

BFAST	LUNCH	DINNER

SNACKS	EXERCISE

OUTFIT

IMPORTANT NOTE

SAT

MY TASKS

....
....
....
....

BFAST	LUNCH	DINNER

OUTFIT

SUN

MY TASKS

....
....
....
....

BFAST	LUNCH	DINNER

OUTFIT

WEEKLY REVIEW

NO. OF GOALS ACHIEVED?...............
LESSONS LEARNED?

....
....
....

HIGHLIGHTS THIS WEEK?

....
....
....

AM I HAPPY WITH THE RESULT?

DATE	WEEK

MY GOALS | DONE

.... ☐
.... ☐
.... ☐
.... ☐
.... ☐
.... ☐
.... ☐
.... ☐

MY TASKS

....
....
....
....
....
....
....
....

BFAST	LUNCH	DINNER

SNACKS	EXERCISE

OUTFIT

IMPORTANT NOTE

MY STRATEGIES

....
....
....
....
....
....
....

MY TASKS

....
....
....
....
....
....
....

BFAST	LUNCH	DINNER

SNACKS	EXERCISE

OUTFIT

IMPORTANT NOTE

SHOPPING LIST

MY TASKS

....
....
....
....
....
....
....

BFAST	LUNCH	DINNER

SNACKS	EXERCISE

OUTFIT

IMPORTANT NOTE

MY TASKS

THU

....
....
....
....
....
....

BFAST	LUNCH	DINNER

SNACKS	EXERCISE

OUTFIT

IMPORTANT NOTE

THINGS I SHOULD TAKE NOTES OF

....
....
....
....
....
....
....

MY TASKS

FRI

....
....
....
....
....
....

BFAST	LUNCH	DINNER

SNACKS	EXERCISE

OUTFIT

IMPORTANT NOTE

....
....
....
....
....
....

MY TASKS

SAT

....
....
....
....

BFAST	LUNCH	DINNER

OUTFIT

MY TASKS

SUN

....
....
....
....

BFAST	LUNCH	DINNER

OUTFIT

WEEKLY REVIEW

NO. OF GOALS ACHIEVED?..............
LESSONS LEARNED?
....
....
....

HIGHLIGHTS THIS WEEK?
....
....
....

AM I HAPPY WITH THE RESULT?

DATE	WEEK

MY GOALS · DONE

- .... ☐
- .... ☐
- .... ☐
- .... ☐
- .... ☐
- .... ☐
- .... ☐
- .... ☐
- .... ☐

MY TASKS

- ....
- ....
- ....
- ....
- ....
- ....

BFAST	LUNCH	DINNER

SNACKS	EXERCISE

OUTFIT

IMPORTANT NOTE

MY STRATEGIES

- ....
- ....
- ....
- ....
- ....
- ....
- ....

MY TASKS

- ....
- ....
- ....
- ....
- ....
- ....

BFAST	LUNCH	DINNER

SNACKS	EXERCISE

OUTFIT

IMPORTANT NOTE

SHOPPING LIST

MY TASKS

- ....
- ....
- ....
- ....
- ....
- ....
- ....

BFAST	LUNCH	DINNER

SNACKS	EXERCISE

OUTFIT

IMPORTANT NOTE

THU

MY TASKS
....
....
....
....
....
....
....

BFAST	LUNCH	DINNER

SNACKS	EXERCISE

OUTFIT

IMPORTANT NOTE

THINGS I SHOULD TAKE NOTES OF
....
....
....
....
....
....
....
....
....

FRI

MY TASKS
....
....
....
....
....
....
....

BFAST	LUNCH	DINNER

SNACKS	EXERCISE

OUTFIT

IMPORTANT NOTE

....
....
....
....
....
....
....
....

SAT

MY TASKS
....
....
....
....

BFAST	LUNCH	DINNER

OUTFIT

SUN

MY TASKS
....
....
....
....

BFAST	LUNCH	DINNER

OUTFIT

WEEKLY REVIEW
NO. OF GOALS ACHIEVED?..............
LESSONS LEARNED?
....
....
....

HIGHLIGHTS THIS WEEK?
....
....
....

AM I HAPPY WITH THE RESULT?

DATE	WEEK

MY GOALS | DONE

.... ☐
.... ☐
.... ☐
.... ☐
.... ☐
.... ☐
.... ☐
.... ☐
.... ☐

MY TASKS

....
....
....
....
....
....
....

BFAST	LUNCH	DINNER

SNACKS	EXERCISE

OUTFIT

IMPORTANT NOTE

MY STRATEGIES

....
....
....
....
....
....

MY TASKS

....
....
....
....
....
....
....

BFAST	LUNCH	DINNER

SNACKS	EXERCISE

OUTFIT

IMPORTANT NOTE

SHOPPING LIST

....
....
....
....
....
....
....

MY TASKS

....
....
....
....
....
....
....

BFAST	LUNCH	DINNER

SNACKS	EXERCISE

OUTFIT

IMPORTANT NOTE

THU

MY TASKS

....
....
....
....
....
....
....
....

BFAST	LUNCH	DINNER

SNACKS	EXERCISE

OUTFIT

IMPORTANT NOTE

FRI

MY TASKS

....
....
....
....
....
....
....
....

BFAST	LUNCH	DINNER

SNACKS	EXERCISE

OUTFIT

IMPORTANT NOTE

SAT

MY TASKS

....
....
....
....
....

BFAST	LUNCH	DINNER

OUTFIT

SUN

MY TASKS

....
....
....
....
....

BFAST	LUNCH	DINNER

OUTFIT

THINGS I SHOULD TAKE NOTES OF

....
....
....
....
....
....
....
....
....
....
....
....
....
....
....

WEEKLY REVIEW

NO. OF GOALS ACHIEVED?..................
LESSONS LEARNED?

....
....
....

HIGHLIGHTS THIS WEEK?

....
....
....

AM I HAPPY WITH THE RESULT?

DATE	WEEK

MY GOALS — DONE

- .... ☐
- .... ☐
- .... ☐
- .... ☐
- .... ☐
- .... ☐
- .... ☐
- .... ☐

MY TASKS

- ....
- ....
- ....
- ....
- ....
- ....

BFAST	LUNCH	DINNER

SNACKS	EXERCISE

OUTFIT

IMPORTANT NOTE

MY STRATEGIES

- ....
- ....
- ....
- ....
- ....
- ....
- ....
- ....

MY TASKS

- ....
- ....
- ....
- ....
- ....
- ....
- ....

BFAST	LUNCH	DINNER

SNACKS	EXERCISE

OUTFIT

IMPORTANT NOTE

SHOPPING LIST

- .... | ....
- .... | ....
- .... | ....
- .... | ....
- .... | ....
- .... | ....
- .... | ....

MY TASKS

- ....
- ....
- ....
- ....
- ....
- ....
- ....

BFAST	LUNCH	DINNER

SNACKS	EXERCISE

OUTFIT

IMPORTANT NOTE

THU

MY TASKS

....
....
....
....
....
....
....

BFAST	LUNCH	DINNER

SNACKS	EXERCISE

OUTFIT

IMPORTANT NOTE

THINGS I SHOULD TAKE NOTES OF

....
....
....
....
....
....
....
....
....
....
....
....
....
....
....
....
....
....

FRI

MY TASKS

....
....
....
....
....
....
....

BFAST	LUNCH	DINNER

SNACKS	EXERCISE

OUTFIT

IMPORTANT NOTE

SAT

MY TASKS

....
....
....
....

BFAST	LUNCH	DINNER

OUTFIT

SUN

MY TASKS

....
....
....
....

BFAST	LUNCH	DINNER

OUTFIT

WEEKLY REVIEW

NO. OF GOALS ACHIEVED?..............
LESSONS LEARNED?

....
....
....

HIGHLIGHTS THIS WEEK?

....
....
....

AM I HAPPY WITH THE RESULT?

DATE	WEEK

MY GOALS | DONE

- .... ☐
- .... ☐
- .... ☐
- .... ☐
- .... ☐
- .... ☐
- .... ☐
- .... ☐
- .... ☐

MY TASKS

- ....
- ....
- ....
- ....
- ....
- ....
- ....
- ....

BFAST	LUNCH	DINNER

SNACKS	EXERCISE

OUTFIT

IMPORTANT NOTE

MY STRATEGIES

- ....
- ....
- ....
- ....
- ....
- ....
- ....

MY TASKS

- ....
- ....
- ....
- ....
- ....
- ....
- ....

BFAST	LUNCH	DINNER

SNACKS	EXERCISE

OUTFIT

IMPORTANT NOTE

SHOPPING LIST

- ....
- ....
- ....
- ....
- ....
- ....
- ....

MY TASKS

- ....
- ....
- ....
- ....
- ....
- ....
- ....

BFAST	LUNCH	DINNER

SNACKS	EXERCISE

OUTFIT

IMPORTANT NOTE

MY TASKS

THU

....
....
....
....
....
....
....

BFAST	LUNCH	DINNER

SNACKS	EXERCISE

OUTFIT

IMPORTANT NOTE

THINGS I SHOULD TAKE NOTES OF

....
....
....
....
....
....
....
....
....

MY TASKS

FRI

....
....
....
....
....
....
....

BFAST	LUNCH	DINNER

SNACKS	EXERCISE

OUTFIT

IMPORTANT NOTE

....
....
....
....
....
....
....

MY TASKS

SAT

....
....
....
....

BFAST	LUNCH	DINNER

OUTFIT

MY TASKS

SUN

....
....
....
....

BFAST	LUNCH	DINNER

OUTFIT

WEEKLY REVIEW

NO. OF GOALS ACHIEVED?...............
LESSONS LEARNED?

....
....
....

HIGHLIGHTS THIS WEEK?

....
....
....

AM I HAPPY WITH THE RESULT?

Made in the USA
Las Vegas, NV
14 August 2021